About
building

Ladybird

Learning Points

This book is designed to introduce young children to the idea of reading.

Learning to read requires many more skills than just decoding words. Children need to learn what a word is, and that reading goes from left to right.

The detailed pictures will give your child clues to what the words say, but most beginning readers will learn the text by heart when the book is repeated several times. This is a normal part of learning to read.

As you go through the book with your child, talk about the pictures and read the text out loud. Move your finger from left to right underneath the words as you say them. One word from the sentence is printed under the picture. Tell your child what the word says and see if he or she can find it in the sentence. Recognizing the shapes of different words is another important part of reading.

If your child is not ready for reading, don't force him or her. Simply enjoy the pictures and the story together.

Acknowledgment
The publishers would like to thank John Dillow
for the cover illustration.

LADYBIRD BOOKS, INC.
Auburn, Maine 04210
Published by LADYBIRD BOOKS LTD.
Loughborough, Leicestershire, U.K.
LADYBIRD and the associated pictorial
device are trademarks of Ladybird Books Ltd.

Printed in Canada

Ladybird Books Inc., Auburn, Maine 04210, U.S.A.
Published by Ladybird Books Ltd., Loughborough, Leicestershire, U.K.

© LADYBIRD BOOKS LTD. 1995
LADYBIRD and the associated pictorial device are trademarks of Ladybird Books Ltd.

Printed in Canada

About
building

by JACQUELINE HARDING

illustrated by STUART TROTTER

Ladybird

Two people came to measure the ground before the building began.

building

First a big shovel came
and scooped up the
earth.

shovel

Everyone wore a hard hat. Watch out for that crane!

crane

Round and round went the cement mixer.

cement mixer

The bricklayers built the walls. There were so many bricks!

bricks

The builders checked the plans. The school building was going well.

A bulldozer made the ground level.

bulldozer

A big shovel loaded
a dump truck.

truck

windows

The roof was almost finished.

roof

The steamroller made
the playground
smooth.

steamroller

The painters painted inside and outside.

The school was ready for some children!